EVERYTHING THEY NEVER TOLD YOU ABOUT RETIREMENT

The New Rules for RETIRING RICH Without the BS, Big Words and Boring Lectures

By
Joe Wirbick

Everything They Never Told You About Retirement
The New Rules for Retiring Rich Without the BS, Big Words and Boring Lectures

www.WirbickResource.com

Printed in the United States of America
First Printing: June 2016

Published by Paradigm Impact Group
info@ParadigmImpactGroup.com

ISBN: 978-0-9977072-0-5

Advisory services offered through J. W. Cole Advisors, Inc. ("JWCA"). Sequinox and JWCA are unaffiliated entities. The information in this book is provided for educational purposes only and should not be construed as insurance, securities, ERISA, tax, investment, mortgage or legal advice. Although care has been taken in preparing this material and presenting it accurately, the author disclaims any express or implied warranty as to the accuracy of any materials contained herein and any liability with respect to it. Interested parties should consult and rely upon their own financial advisors regarding their particular situation and the concepts presented here.

The information contained herein does not purport to be a complete description and any opinions expressed are solely those of the author, Joe Wirbick and not J. W. Cole Advisors, Inc. This information is not intended to be a solicitation or offer to buy, sell or hold any security; nor is it intended to be a recommendation to implement any investment strategy. All investments and investment strategies contain risk including the potential loss of principal and prior to making any investment decision you should consult with your financial advisor. Past performance is no guarantee of future results and any examples used are hypothetical for illustrative purposes, actual client results will vary.

Some factual and historical pieces of data included in this book can be referenced at: www.IRS.gov and www.taxfoundation.org

I dedicate this book to my father who always taught me that "Nothing is impossible!" Thank you Dad, you were right.

TABLE OF CONTENTS

PREFACE

A financial advisor is vacationing in Mexico. One morning he is walking on the beach and spies a Mexican fisherman coming to shore. The advisor approaches the fisherman, and sees he has caught two big blue fin tuna and has them in his small rowboat.

The advisor meets the fisherman on the shore and asks what he plans to do with the fish. "I caught these fish to feed my family and friends, Señor," the fisherman replies.

"Don't you know the value of the fish you have caught?" the advisor asks. "Are you going to go back out and fish more today?"

"No, Señor, I am done fishing for the day," the fisherman replies.

"What? Why?" asks the advisor. "Don't you realize it is still early in the day? You could go back out and catch more. These fish are worth a lot of money!" exclaims the advisor.

"No, Señor, I am heading home right now," the fisherman tells him.

"Why are you heading home?" the advisor asks—"for what?"

"Oh, Señor, I am going home to be with my family. I am going to play with my kids, take a siesta in the afternoon, and enjoy the fish for dinner with my wife. Then I will go into town and play guitar with my amigos and dance with my beautiful wife," the fisherman replies. "That is my normal day."

"No, you don't understand," the advisor says. "I am a financial advisor and I understand business and money. You could sell those two fish you have and get enough money to buy another boat. You could then hire a friend to fish with you, and in a short time you would have enough money for a whole fleet of fishing boats," the advisor continued. "Soon after that you could open up restaurants in America and supply the fish directly to your customers' plates. You could own your own trucks to deliver the fish to your restaurants. Before you knew it, you'd be worth millions."

"Wow, Señor, that sounds incredible," the fisherman replied. "How long would all this take?"

"You could probably accomplish all that in as few as fifteen to twenty years."

"Fifteen to twenty years!" the fisherman exclaimed. "And what would I be able to do once I earn these millions after working hard for fifteen to twenty years?" the fisherman asked.

"Well, then," the advisor replied, "you could get yourself a little place by the ocean, have time to play with your grandkids, siesta in the afternoon, go to town to play guitar with your amigos, and dance with your wife."

I hope the opening parable caught your attention. I want you to continue to think about the story of the Mexican fisherman. I want it to stay with you throughout the entire book. You see, we all have different ideas about retirement. We all have our own wants and needs. It is unfortunate that those wants and needs typically revolve around money.

We feel that money is the answer. However, for the Mexican fisherman, money played a very small role in his life. Yet one long, far-off day when we reach retirement, many of us aspire to a life such as his.

I hope this book helps you on your journey to wherever your dreams may take you. And as part of my commitment to help, I've put together a great set of resources for you that will be referenced in a few places throughout this book. My goal is to simply provide more information for you and to help you achieve your goals. There is NO FEE for this set of resources, it is an extension of my ongoing efforts to serve people just like you.

Simply go to
www.WirbickResource.com
and I'll be happy to give you access.

INTRODUCTION

It's not what you know you know, it's what you know that just ain't so

~ Mark Twain ~

Have you ever wondered how other people do it? How so many people make it look so effortless? You see them enjoying themselves, traveling, playing golf, relaxing. Does it seem like the dream of retirement may be out of your reach?

Hi, my name is Joe Wirbick and I am here to tell you that you, too, may achieve retirement success! You may leave that job where you have been killing yourself for your whole life. You may find that "extra time" in the day that you have been searching for all these years, and you may finally travel to all those wonderful places you have been putting on your "bucket" list. You may do all these things, and I am here to tell you how to plan to do them the *Right* way.

I have done all the hard work. I have spent the past twenty years helping many people achieve their dream of a successful retirement. Through my decades of research and data collection, I have assembled the best and most financially rewarding methods to plan for a truly successful retirement. I have learned the strategies that have allowed my clients to attain the reality of a fun and fulfilling retirement. And you know what? None of them are too difficult or out of your reach.

I have compiled the notes that I've gathered over the years and boiled them down to seven steps to plan retirement success. I believe anyone can achieve these results, as long as they are willing to follow these steps.

By following these seven steps, you too may enjoy financial independence in your latter years.

I am going to open my knowledge bank of "insider" secrets that no one has been likely willing to share with you, showing you how you can grow your money faster than you ever thought possible. I will demystify those cloudy and difficult to understand IRS rules, which may permit you to avoid unnecessary taxes, fees, and penalties. In my professional experience I have seen that by following these seven steps and committing to retiring well, you may experience unlimited success one day. Keeping the vision of what you want your retirement to look like always in mind improves your opportunity to get to those beaches and greens before you know it!!

Don't simply retire from something;
have something to retire to
~ Harry Emerson Fosdick ~

A LITTLE ABOUT THE BOOK

I have laid the book out in seven chapters, each of which covers a distinct step in my formula for retirement success. When you combine them, they will help ensure that you have a happy and fruitful retirement. The initial chapter is your introduction. There is no need to read the other chapters in chronological order. Find the one that speaks to you best and begin there! I am also giving you the link I mentioned in the preface to my strategic online resource (www.WirbickResource.com) that will assist you further along your journey.

In Chapter 1, we will start by deciding what you want to get out of retirement. It is important to begin with the end in mind. Chapter 2 lays the groundwork for beginning your savings plan. In Chapter 3, we will move on to learn how taxes will affect your future dollars. Chapter 4 covers the secrets to maximizing Social Security; there is more to it than you ever imagined. In Chapter 5, we will cover one of the greatest savings strategies of wealthy people. In Chapter 6, we will examine the pros and cons of home ownership (we will especially cover why it is not a bank). Finally, we will cover my favorite step in Chapter 7, in which I will lay out some of my best-kept secrets to a more fulfilling life and why you may not want to wait until retirement to get started.

The trouble with retirement is that you never get a day off

~ Abe Lemons ~

Are you ready? Then let's get started…

WHO AM I?

I have spent the last 20 years devoting my professional talent to working with retirees, and I have learned the ways in which many successful people ultimately fail during retirement. It is my goal to ensure that doesn't happen to you. I came into the industry initially not knowing exactly what I wanted to do when I grew up. All I knew for sure was that I loved working with people, I enjoyed sharing my knowledge, and I had a passion for making a difference. However, I came from very humble beginnings.

I grew up in a family of five, in which I was the youngest and only boy. Both my parents worked two jobs in order to support us. My mother was always a waitress, going from restaurant to restaurant, working hard on her feet for 12-14 hours a day. My father was a compressor repairman and all around "jack of all trades." Typically, he came home from his full time job, just in time to leave for a part time one.

Thus, I sort of raised myself. I spent a lot of time in front of the TV in the 70s and 80s, dreaming of a better life for myself. I knew, deep down inside, that one day I would achieve greatness. I would not work my fingers to the bone 100 hours a week like my folks did. I would find a way to achieve true financial success.

My first job was selling dried floral arrangements at local flea markets. I was 15 and hungry for a career. My boss was amazed, and said I was her best employee ever. Her favorite line to describe me was that "I could sell ice cubes to Eskimos!" I loved working with the public and making them happy.

I worked all through high school, from the flea markets to being a busboy in high-end restaurants, honing my skills with the public, even when they were unhappy. I had a knack with people.

I graduated high school near the top of my class and joined the Army immediately. I loved languages and had heard the best language school was in California at DLI, The Defense Language Institute. However, you had to be in the military to go there. My family has a long and illustrious military history. My mother's maiden name was Custer and we have had a Custer in every major battle since the founding of this great country of ours—General George being the most infamous of those. So, I signed up for the Army and gave them the next four years of my life.

I tested highly on my language entrance exams and was told I would be learning Korean. Korean? I knew nothing about Korean. I had already learned Spanish, German, some Japanese, and was pretty well versed in English, but Korean? Nope, no clue. Like everything else in life until that point, I just accepted that was my fate and dove headlong into a new adventure.

I loved everything about translating Korean, taking something that was confusing and incomprehensible and making it crystal clear with my knowledge. As much as I loved the translation aspect of my career however, unfortunately, I did not love the life of an enlisted soldier. I could not stop myself from questioning why we were doing things the way we were told to do them. For anyone who has been in the military, you know it is not our place to question why. We are simply supposed to obey.

That was not easy for me, and after four years, I decided that I should continue my career outside the armed forces.

When I got out, I was not alone. I now had a wife and a newborn, which meant I needed to get to work. I took the first job that came along. My father-in-law worked for a small tire company and they needed a driver/salesman. I had no desire to drive a truck, but the sales part sounded promising. Glamorous? No, but it paid the bills. Unfortunately, the job entailed far more driving than it did sales. I spent the next three months driving a box truck over 1,000 miles a week delivering tires. It definitely paid the bills, but that was about it. I was miserable. It was summer. My truck did not have air conditioning and I was hot.

I knew I had responsibilities to meet; I had to take care of my family. However, I was not happy at all. I had just spent 4 years in the Army, not really enjoying myself. I had made myself a promise then never to work somewhere that I did not enjoy, but here I was doing just that. I began looking for a way out.

I remember the day my life changed. It was a Thursday in late June and I had already driven over 850 miles that week and was on my way home. Traffic was miserable, the heat was unbearable, and I was not in a good mood. I pulled up to a stop light and noticed the car in front of me. It was a brand new Audi TT convertible. The man driving it was wearing a blue suit and talking on his cell phone. That was what I wanted. I wanted to be a businessman, not a truck driver. I wanted to work at an office, start my own company, and become the success I always knew I would be. At that moment, I realized I was not going to achieve that while behind the wheel of that truck.

A few weeks prior to this, a family friend had said he felt I would be great in the financial services industry. He said that I had a way with people and he believed I could do really well. I listened half-heartedly and dismissed the idea. What did I know about selling investments?

Back to the hot truck and beautiful Audi: I can still see that car almost twenty years later. It will be burned in my mind's eye forever. When I got back to the shop, I went to my boss's office and told him I was resigning. He asked what I was going to do. I told him I was going into the financial services industry. He laughed. He actually laughed. He said I would be back in less than a month begging for my job. He said that was an industry fraught with failure, and that only a fool would give up the position I had, and the opportunities ahead of me, to sell investments. I stood up and walked out.

I believe it was his words that kept me from giving up early on when things got tough. I wanted to prove him wrong so badly and, man, am I glad I did. Nearly twenty years, four Audis, and three self made companies later, I am so happy I saw that Audi when I did.

CHAPTER 1
HOW TO MAKE YOUR OWN REALITY

If you don't know where you are going,
you'll end up someplace else
~ Yogi Berra ~

How to Make Your Own Right Reality

First, you need to decide what you want to get out of retirement. What does retirement mean to you?

Before I formed Sequinox, my advisory firm, I sat down in my tiny 400 square foot office in the basement of the building I was renting, and wrote what I expected to get out of it, not only the financial benefits, but also the personal. I wrote how many new clients I wanted to bring on and how many assets I wanted to bring in the first year. I then wrote down my personal goals: work only four days a week and take four weeks' vacation a year. When I was done, I sat back and stared at what looked like impossible goals. How could I expect to do all those amazing things?

Guess what? It worked. Now, don't get me wrong, I'm not saying that it happened overnight; I had to work hard to achieve those goals, but I never would have come close had I not written them down first. A goal is just an idea until you write it down and act upon it.

I am now writing this book in my 3000 square foot office in the 55,000 square foot office building that I own! Again, dreams are just those, dreams, until you write them down and act on them.

So, let's get some of yours down on paper. I have provided blank lines to facilitate the process.

Start by closing your eyes and imagining that tomorrow is the first day of your retirement. What are you going to do? Sleep in late, then go out for a celebratory breakfast? Relax on the front porch? Start checking off that honey-do list? Will you begin volunteer work? What about the next day, and the day after that? Will you start traveling more? Will you write that book you have always said you were going to write? Now…open your eyes.

Begin writing down everything that will make your retirement the most personally fulfilling. Dream big; don't leave anything out. If you want to travel around the world, write it down. If you never want to cook again and eat out all the time, put that down; if you really want a brand new Porsche 911 turbo Cabriolet in which to cruise around town, spell that out.

What the mind can conceive and believe, and the heart desire, you can achieve

~ Dr. Norman Vincent Peale ~

Do not—I repeat—DO NOT—short-change yourself. This is your future to design, your story to write. If you go small, you will get small. Henry Ford said it best when he said, "Whether we think we can or we can't, we are right." I want you to pour out your greatest desires right there on the paper—write it all out. Take your time with this. You can revisit it again and again. It may take you a few days to jot down your dreams. That's Okay. In my opinion this is ***the*** most important step in all that we do. Do not skip this one or it may not work—or worse, it may work, but not in the way you wanted it to.

Obstacles are things a person sees when he takes his eyes off his goal

~ E. Joseph Cossman ~

Great, so now you have your ideas down on paper. Are you happy with them? If not, change them; redo them until you're content.

I recommend involving your spouse or partner at this stage. I think the power of one mind is incredible—the power of two together is unstoppable. Get her (him) on board, have her (him) share what she (he) wants out of retirement, because it may be different, and that's okay. Those differences are what can unite us.

After you are happy with your list, let's move on.

Now you know what you want out of your retirement. You can see it, smell it, and maybe even taste it. That's great; it may help you over the years as you journey ever closer to realizing your dreams. The next six steps are the building blocks to achieve those dreams. At any time along the way, come back and revise them. That is what life is about. Making plans, living them, and then making new ones. Maybe you'll find that what you wanted today is not what gets you excited a few years from now. What is important is that you come back and write it down again. There can be incredible power in this process. Keep it going, because I think you will find it will be well worth it in the end. We will refer back to your list throughout the process; make sure to keep it handy.

The greater danger for most of us lies not in setting our aim too high and falling short; but in setting our aim too low, and achieving our mark

~ Michelangelo Buonarroti ~

CHAPTER 2
START NOW

The beginning is always today

~ Mary Shelley ~

Tom and Joan have been clients of mine for almost 20 years. Both are hard-working, blue collar folks. Neither of them have a college degree, but what they never received in book learning, they have far surpassed in real world living. Tom and Joan have both been saving for their retirement since they started at their companies. As soon as they were allowed to begin their 401(k)s, they put away some of their earnings. While those initial contributions were small, time and a little thing called compounding interest made up for that.

When it comes to saving for retirement, I want you to start today—not tomorrow, not next week. Now! Do it now. The earlier you begin to save, the less you have to put away. Ben Franklin said it best when he coined the phrase, "A penny saved is a penny earned." No truer words have been spoken, but unfortunately, saving pennies won't get us far in today's economy; however, it is amazing that when we put just a little bit away over a long time, we can have more money than we ever dreamed.

However, before we get into saving you enough money for your dream retirement, let's cover a checklist of a few steps you need to take to protect yourself along the way (see www.Wirbick-Resource.com to go through this list yourself).

People tend to overlook one of the most important areas when planning for retirement: protecting their assets. I'm not referring to market loss protection; I mean lawsuit protection. Did you know that there are over 15 million lawsuits filed annually in the U.S. today, and that 55% of the time the plaintiff (that is the person suing you!) wins? Those numbers frighten me.

Whenever a new client comes into my office, one of the first questions I ask him or her is, "What kind of lawsuit protection do you have in place in case someone tries to sue you?" I typically get a blank stare in return. The majority of my new clients have overlooked this area. In some cases I am dealing with people who have assets in the millions, and yet they have not taken the time to ensure that they are adequately protected from some nut out there who is hell-bent on suing them for all they are worth.

Therefore, in my opinion the first thing you need to do is look at your auto and homeowner's insurance declarations pages. These will list what kind of protection you have in place now.

I see the late night commercials on TV that tout cut-rate car insurance. These companies offer you the cheapest coverage possible and I often see people fall for the pitches. This could turn out to be a *very* bad idea, especially for people who have already accumulated any assets, or for people who want to make sure they are protected in case of an accident.

We want to focus on your liability protection, so look for numbers that may say 50/100 or 100/300. This indicates the extent to which you are protected should you be involved in an accident. The first number shows how much money your policy will cover per person, and the second shows your total coverage for the accident in the thousands (50/100 equals $50,000 per person/$100,000 per accident).

For example, say you are driving a friend around town and you cause an accident. Let's assume the other car has two passengers, and all of you end up going to the hospital. Fortunately, no one dies. However, you all spend a few days in the hospital getting patched up. Assume you all have hospital bills of approximately $100,000. If your policy limits are 50/100, it will only cover up to $50,000 per person (remember: in this case each has a bill of $100,000) or a total of $100,000 for the occurrence (your total is $400,000). So, your policy will only cover $100,000 total. Where is the money coming from to cover the rest of the claims? Unfortunately, out of your pocket, and if you don't have the money now, they could garnish your wages for the rest of your life. That may make it pretty difficult to live, let alone save for your retirement.

After you have decided upon what is the appropriate coverage for you (typically 250/500), you may now want to go a step further. Ask your agent to supply you with a quote for umbrella coverage. No, this is not in case it rains. This covers you, your cars, your house, and maybe even your boat if you have one, perhaps up to a minimum of $1,000,000. You can buy more if you feel you need it.

I usually recommend that my clients get at least $1 million of umbrella coverage. Typically the cost for this is very minimal, on average approximately $12 a month, less than a few trips to Starbucks. However, the coverage might save you, and your savings, for the rest of your life!!

Okay, so now you have your liability covered, let's move on to cash protection. I see many clients who hoard cash in their savings and checking accounts. When I ask them why, most clients respond that it is their rainy day fund.

Great, I love emergency funds; they're very important. However, too much of a good thing is still too much. I recommend that you keep approximately six months of expenses in your cash account at all times, up to a maximum of twelve months.

The downside to this is that these accounts typically offer little to no growth on your money. If your monthly expenses are $3,000, this could mean having up to $18,000 in your cash account, or if your expenses are $6,000, you could have as much as $36,000 earning nothing!

Now that we have covered a few basic ways to help protect the assets you hold today, and the future assets I know you are going to accumulate, let us move on to actually putting some money away for the future.

In my opinion, the best place to start saving for your retirement is at work. Most companies offer savings plans, such as 401(k)s. I believe these are a great first step to investing. They offer a broad mix of investments and an easy way to save: payroll deductions. I believe most people fail to save any money because they do not pay themselves first.

What does it mean to pay yourself first? This means that you have the money taken out of your paycheck before it hits your bank account. You pay yourself first, rather than others. This ensures you are putting away for the future every month. Systematic investment plans are typically the most long term successful plans.

One convenient way to way to pay yourself first is to have your company do it for you.

Your company may even match your funds. I believe this can yield the biggest returns your money will ever make. When your company matches your contribution, you have immediately doubled your investment! With a 6% return, it normally would take over 12 years to accomplish the same thing. Further, that's assuming you make 6% and never have a negative return, two very difficult things to accomplish.

If you are young and reading this book, great job: you are well on your way and have taken a step towards having an enormous advantage over your older counterparts.

Let's assume you just got out of college and have landed your first job. You are 22 years old and earn $3,000 per month. You know you want to save for retirement, so you defer 10% into your 401(k). Because it is a traditional 401(k), the contributions will be pre-tax and you will be saving around $300 a month. If your investments return 6% over your life and you never get a raise (not sure why you are still working there) or increase the percentage you save, you will have saved **$753,849** at age 65—not bad!

Now, let's assume you don't start right away. You decide you would rather wait until you're making more money, until you're more established. Let's face it, saving can be hard. Just look at all that cool stuff out there you can buy.

Therefore, you put off saving until age 35. You have worked hard, landed a few promotions, and doubled your pay. Now you begin to save 10% of your pay, which yields the same 6%. That is the equivalent of $600 a month because you are now making

$6,000. You are putting away twice as much per month than you would have at age 22, so it was okay to wait, right?

Wrong! When you reach age 65, you will have accumulated only **$317,843**, less than half as much as your 22-year-old self did. How can this be? How could those 13 years cost you over ***$436,000***?

Compounding interest; that's how. You lost all those years and all that time your money could have been growing with the help of compounding interest. Albert Einstein called compounding interest "The eighth wonder of the world" because of its ability to take small amounts of money and make them grow over an extended time. It's sort of how my stomach seems to grow over the holiday season.

So, as this example illustrates, it may be that your best first place to save is at work. Your work may offer a retirement plan; if so, sign up now! Paying yourself first is one potential way to ensure success.

Therefore, you must begin contributing to your company's plan. We will cover the type of plan you should seek in Chapter 3. For now, just sign up. Don't wait. The majority of my most successful clients' largest assets are their company's retirement plans. These monies are the basis for making your retirement a reality.

Once you are contributing to your company plan at the level appropriate for you, you may want to look elsewhere for additional investments. As much as I may love your company's plan, it includes some strict rules about accessing your funds early, and you probably will not have much control over the investments they choose. This is where a self-directed IRA may come into play. I will cover this more in a bit.

Not all companies offer plans. If yours does not, don't worry, because you have many other options. You can set up your own self-directed saving plan, and you can start these plans at many online investment sites, or through a qualified financial advisor.

Similar to a company-sponsored plan, this allows you to begin saving for retirement on your own. I recommend using an automatic monthly deferment from your bank account. Again, pay yourself first. If you don't, no one else ever may.

You may decide to open a simple taxable savings account or an IRA. I recommend starting with an IRA, because there are many tax benefits to these plans, although they do have some strict rules you need to follow. We won't go too deep into their finer points right now, as we'll cover IRAs in depth in Chapter 3. Just know this money is meant for retirement, so don't expect to access the funds early without a significant IRS tax penalty.

I recommend starting with 10% of your pay. That may sound like a lot. However, it is going to hurt that much more when you are forced to continue working long after your peers have stopped because they had more discipline than you did.

If you do start with 10%, bravo, I believe you're on the right track. If not, that's okay, because strategies are designed to help you plan to reach this higher level.

Every time you get a raise, it is my belief you need to give your future self one as well. Increase your savings amount along with the raise. This can be a painless way to invest more money for the future. When you combine this with compounding interest, your retirement date could be closer than ever.

Once you have established this savings plan, you need to stick with it. It will become second nature before you know it, and you will wonder why you didn't start sooner.

You may choose to do all of this on your own. If so, you may find there are some great organizations out there that work with individuals who want to handle their own investments. You may achieve a high level of satisfaction knowing you did it yourself.

Of course, as a financial advisor, I would not recommend this route. Typically in everything that I do, I find someone who has already mastered that area of expertise and pay them for their advice. In everything you want, it helps to find someone who may help get you there faster.

A financial professional can assist in selecting which investments will help you achieve greater financial success through the years. Make sure you understand how s/he is compensated; a financial advisor can be paid in many ways.

Financial professionals receive compensation in two basic ways; commissions or advisory fees/planning fees. Each form of compensation relates directly to the professional's title and job description and requires its own set of licenses, affiliations, registrations, and regulations.

When selecting a financial professional to aid in asset planning and management, be aware that you can choose from more than 600,000 financial advisors and insurance agents registered in the U.S. Therefore, it's important to understand whom you are hiring and how you pay for his/her services.

Fee Only

Let's take a look at the fee-only advisor. This individual will likely put together a financial plan for you and charge an hourly or flat fee for that advice. It can be a broad plan that outlines strategies to save for retirement, or a comprehensive financial plan that covers college savings, estate planning, tax management, and retirement planning as well. You can look at the fee as a measure that allows the advisor to make unbiased recommendations that are designed to suit you best, rather than developing a plan that will earn commissions on the investments recommended.

If the advisor is only a planner, this may be where your involvement with this individual ends, as s/he may not be licensed or may not wish to help implement the plan for you. You may also see this as a way to ensure the advice is what's best for you, and that it isn't designed to benefit the planner's bottom line.

Many planners will offer ongoing advice as you implement the plan with other financial professionals to help make sure you stay on track with the original recommendations. You can look at this advisor in the same way you look at an architect: s/he designs the building and may oversee its construction, but never picks up a hammer and saw.

If the advisor does help you implement the plan, you need to understand that the fee-only portion of the advice may end at that time, and you may be heading into a commission relationship. The advisor has to disclose this fully before any further service begins, and you should feel comfortable asking why s/he recommended certain investment products over others. You should be able to see what the advisor can charge you by simply reading his/her Form ADV, Part 2. The advisor needs to give this to you before the engagement can begin.

Before choosing any advisor, I recommend that you check him/her out the best you can prior to engaging his/her services. You can search many sites online to check for clean records and proper licenses. In order to charge for advice, advisors need to have a series 65 or 66 or qualify for a licensing exemption and be registered currently in your state or qualify for an exemption for registration. You can visit the FINRA and SEC websites to begin background checks. In addition, don't forget about recommendations and referrals from colleagues, and friends or family you trust.

Most states, in order for financial professionals to carry the title of advisor, they typically must either pass the series 65 or 66 exam, or obtain a highly qualified professional designation, such as the CFP (certified financial planner). Further, the individual must typically be an investment advisor who represents a registered investment advisory firm (also known as an RIA).

These distinctions give advisors the ability to charge you fees for their planning advice, as well as the capacity to charge you a fee based on a percentage of your portfolio assets (whether they manage it directly or solicit it to a third-party money manager). This differs from commission-based representatives, who only charge when they buy or sell assets.

Fee-based representatives may be appealing to people who like the idea that their advisor is not motivated to buy and sell positions just to get paid. The belief is that fee-based advisors will do their best to grow the assets because their compensation is tied directly to the success of the customer's portfolio. Some feel this ties the advisor to the wants and needs of their customers more so than do other compensation models.

After entering an agreement with an advisor, s/he will disclose the fee schedule. This schedule cannot change unless you enter into a new agreement. The advisor also will supply you with an ADV, Part 2b. This will give a history of the advisor's disciplinary background, however, the disciplinary record will include only formal actions taken by the SEC, the states or SRO (Self-Regulatory organizations e.p. FINRA, NFA, etc.) It will not include arbitration or customer complaints that may not have been subject to formal actions. If the adviser is or was a registered broker, there are easy ways to find out out more (see the links at www.WirbickResource.com) and it may be worthwhile to look into them.

The SEC sets maximum amounts that advisors can charge, and it is up to the firm to set its own fees within these limits. These fees are provided in the firm's ADV, so it is in your best interest to look around and see what others are billing.

You should do what is best for you and your hard-earned money, so taking the time upfront, doing your homework, and interviewing multiple professionals who offer different pricing options is a wise way to start. Going in with a list of questions to ask during the interview may help you get the most out of the meeting. This will help you understand the person sitting in front of you better, and may help you pick that one professional you can feel comfortable with for years to come. You can find more information on this at my free resource site www.WirbickResource.com

Financial professionals are required to inform customers how they will receive their compensation. Whether they are required to do so legally or not, it is your responsibility to ask this question up front and have them explain the process to you clearly.

The way a financial professional answers your questions regarding his/her compensation can be a valuable indicator of the type of professional you will be dealing with in the future.

Commission Based

Commission-based financial professionals are paid only when they buy or sell something for you, and the size of the commission is based on the product bought or sold or the amount of principal transacted. They do not make money if you are not active in your portfolio.

Typically, brokers have a set commission range, and the trade confirmation will disclose transaction costs and commissions fully after each transaction is completed. However, it is within your rights to discuss the commission rate prior to having your financial professional conduct transactions on your behalf.

While it is normal to see commission rates of 1-5% (not including the ticket charge), it is sometimes possible to negotiate an alternative commission rate with your advisor.

Many people assume automatically that their financial professional is looking over their portfolio constantly. This may not always be so in the case of a commission-based model. Don't assume anything. Make sure you understand fully what your professional's role will be as it relates to your portfolio.

It may not be possible for the individual to monitor your positions in the market regularly. I have heard numerous clients tell me they thought their previous representative was always looking at the market for them, only to find out that nothing happened unless they initiated contact with their broker.

My recommendation is to state clearly what you expect from your financial professional, and reinforce it from time to time. If you don't communicate with your professional, s/he has no way to know how you want them to work for you.

When you look for a financial professional, I believe you need to find one who not only is qualified and suits your financial model, but also one who works well with your personality. It usually is easier to talk with a professional you like and trust, than with one that you don't.

Now that you have begun saving, and have decided whether to go it alone, or to hire a professional, let's move on to the finer points of how the government will deal with your investments.

Now let's go back to Tom and Joan who I told you about earlier. They had a **goal**; they wanted to retire one day. They also had a **plan**: to start saving at work and continue adding to that pot every month, year after year. Then they realized their **dream** of retiring when that pot had grown to a size they never thought possible!

The question isn't at what age I want to retire,
it's at what income

~ George Foreman ~

CHAPTER 3
TAXES MAY NOT BE GUARANTEED

I am proud to be paying taxes in the United States. The only thing is—I could be just as proud for half the money

~ Arthur Godfrey ~

The One Way to Tax-Free

George and Melinda came to see me just recently. George is about to retire from the company where he has worked for 30 years. Melinda will continue to work, because she is her own boss and loves what she does.

It is such a feeling of accomplishment when your clients achieve their goal of retiring. That feeling is magnified 100 times when those clients retire and live tax free!!

George listened to me 15 years ago and did something that very few people were willing to do. It cost him a lot of money at the time, but if you ask him today if it was worth it, his smile is all the answer you need.

Now let's get a better understanding of how the Government is going to potentially treat all that money we are saving now. Most of us have heard the common phrase that the only certain things in life are "death and taxes," so let's begin to understand better how taxes could affect our savings so that we can attempt to maximize our hard-earned dollars.

I hear people complain all the time about the high taxes we pay in this country. I understand; believe me, I do. However, I also know that what we pay today is a mere fraction of what we have been asked to pay in the past. George Santayana said, "Those who cannot remember the past are condemned to repeat it." Well, I fear that is exactly where we are heading today.

Back in the 1940s, there was a famous Hollywood actor. This gentleman loved to make movies, and he was able to make as many as he wanted, because of his huge success. However, he decided to make only three. Why three, you may wonder? Was it too taxing for him (an inside joke you will get in a moment). Was he too busy? Actually, if you know our tax history, it actually was too taxing.

See, at one time, we had lower tax rates than we do today. Back in 1913, when they first began to levy federal income taxes after the ratification of the 16th amendment, we had a few years of volatile tax rates. They began with a maximum tax of only 7% (wow, those truly were the days!!). Then they skyrocketed to a maximum of 73%! We finally got lower rates in 1925 when maximum tax rates were a mere 25%.

Life was good then, which is why they called it "the Roaring 20s." Unfortunately, it seems people were unprepared for what came next, the Great Depression. The Dow Jones hit its peak in 1930 at 341 points, then plummeted over the next two years to bottom out at a mere 41!

The country went into a panic, people lost jobs, money, and even their lives. The U.S. government responded in a way that they felt would help boost the economy. They raised income taxes from a high of 25% in 1931 to a staggering 63% in 1932. That is a 250% increase, and they didn't stop there. By the official end of the Great Depression, we had top rates of over 88%!

Cut back to our famous actor: he is making movies and along with the fame came a lot of money. When the government is taxing you at the federal level of 88%, and you add in state taxes, you may be taxed over 100%, so you really don't keep much, if any, of your hard-earned money.

So what was our actor's solution? Only make three movies a year and avoid the higher tax brackets. Works well if you can manage it.

Fast forward to 1981, and our famous actor decides Hollywood is no longer for him; he has his eye on the White House. If you haven't figured it out yet, I am speaking of Ronald Reagan. However, do you know that from 1932-1981 taxes topped out at over 70%! It wasn't until Reagan took office that he was able to lower them to 50% in 1982, and then 35% in 1987. They stayed there until 2014, when Congress raised them for the first time in almost 30 years. You see, ultimately, in my opinion it took an individual who felt the pain of high taxes to lower them.

Why am I telling you this story? I surmise you need to understand that our tax rates actually are at all-time historic lows. We have been living in an age where we actually get to keep the majority of our money. This is great! Unfortunately, I think a lot of you are saving as if we are still living in the 70s.

Tax-deductible IRAs (Individual Retirement Accounts) were instituted first with the ERISA act of 1974. I think the idea of the IRA was a great one back in the early 70s. See, the IRA allowed you to put money away for the future without paying any taxes on it today. The taxes were deferred until you retired and withdrew the money. The thought was that you would then be in a much lower tax bracket, and the taxes owed on the money would be significantly less than they were when you were working and saving.

In 1974, when IRAs started, our top tax rate was a whopping 70%. In addition, the space between our tax brackets was only a few thousand dollars. For example, if you made $40,000 you were in the 48% tax bracket, $44,000 and you jumped to the 50% bracket. So, by saving pre-tax money in a tax-deferred IRA, you were able to forgo taxes when they were high. This may have even moved you to a lower tax bracket. We were then told that when we retired, we would finally be in a much lower tax bracket because we would be making less.

If you were lucky enough to retire before Reagan came to office, I believe you probably would have moved to a much lower tax bracket and the IRA would have made a lot of sense. After Reagan however, the IRA seems to have lost its appeal.

Reagan not only lowered taxes, but he also made the spaces between the tax brackets significantly larger. After he took office, the spaces grew from a few thousand to $20, $30, or even $40,000. This changed everything. At that point, the idea of retiring in a lower tax bracket might not become a reality for everyone.

Today, the average family makes approximately $50,000, which places them in the 15% tax bracket, the top of which is $78,000. There is only one lower bracket, the 10%, and you have to make less than $18,000 to qualify for that. Fundamentally, in certain income ranges this cancels out the tax effectiveness of the

IRA. You are putting money away in a 15% bracket and taking it back out in the same bracket.

What is worse is that taxes can always go up! Whenever I have spoken during the past 10 years, I always ask the audience if they think taxes could go up. I always get a unanimous response, that "YES," they believe they will.

Think about it; if we had taxes that exceeded 70% for over 40 years, now that our top bracket is a mere 39.5%, who is to say that our brackets could not return to those levels again?

Today, we are facing government deficits of over $18 trillion! Many believe our tax revenue is not enough to cover our growing government's budget, so they may be forced to do something about it. If they feel they need more revenue, they could always raise taxes.

Think about it. We have over 90 million Baby Boomers facing retirement. We have saved over $20 trillion in IRAs, of which only 1% is in Roth IRAs. If you were running a company that was facing massive deficits, wouldn't you think of ways to bring in more money?

The thinking may be that making a few small tax increases at the time when a large amount of the population is forced to take money out of accounts that have never been taxed could give them the extra money they need to keep going.

If that were to occur, then I think the IRA would hurt, not help you. You might be saying, "I wanted to put money away and not pay taxes at the 15% level, and now I take it out when I'm retired and in a much higher bracket! What? That doesn't make any sense."

Add to that all the growth you may have had on the IRA that hasn't ever been taxed. You could be paying significantly more taxes when you retire than you did while you were working. As we say here in Lancaster County, it is better to pay for the seed than the harvest.

In addition to the risk of paying higher taxes on the money you take out of your IRA in retirement, these dollars could force you to pay excess tax on your social security income. We will cover this in more detail in Chapter 4.

Required Minimum Distribution (RMD)

Maybe some of you are thinking, okay, if taxes are higher, I just won't pull the money out of the IRA. I don't think that makes much sense, given that you're saving it for retirement. However, I do have clients who have pensions and really don't need their IRAs. Unfortunately, the government has already thought of this.

In my opinion when you first opened your IRA, you unknowingly took on a business partner, the U.S. Treasury Department, aka the IRS. Their partnership remains a silent one for years—either until you begin to take money out on your own or are forced to at age 70.5. Because you have been able to grow your money all those years without paying taxes, they have decided that when you reach the age of 70.5, you must begin to take out the money. This may force those people who do not want to spend their IRAs to do precisely that.

If you choose to ignore this requirement, believe me, they will catch up with you sooner or later, and the penalty is 50% of what you were required to take out; moreover, you still have to take the money out and pay taxes on it.

The required distribution is not too large, only approximately 3.75% of the account value the first year. However, each year the required distribution increases.

If you want to calculate what yours would be, you just divide the value of your IRA (found on your statement) as of December

31st of the year before you turn 70.5 by 27.4. Why 27.4? Because that is the number they told us we need to use. As you age, that number gets smaller, and effectively increases the amount of your distribution. You can read more about this on my free retirement resource site www.WirbickResource.com.

I have a client whom we'll call Jim. Jim came into my office the other day with a huge smile on his face. I do love starting meetings with happy clients. I asked him why he was so happy. He then pulled out his last year's tax returns and showed me how we had effectively moved him into a 0% tax bracket.

He was in such a good mood, and was going on and on about how happy he was that he was living such a comfortable life in retirement; he and his wife had just purchased a vacation home in Florida, and they were not paying any income taxes to the IRS. It all seemed too good to be true.

Unfortunately, I knew that it was not too good to be true, but only for the next few years. When Jim reached the age of 70.5, his entire tax picture was going to change in a very dramatic fashion.

You see, Jim was putting off taking any money out of his IRA. He was living on money he had saved in taxable accounts and his Social Security income. Because his distributions from these accounts had very little tax effect, it was not enough to cause his social security to become taxable (we will cover taxes on Social Security income in Chapter 4), so his effective tax actually was $0.

What Jim was not taking into account was how large his tax-deferred IRA was becoming; every year that he put off removing funds from his IRA, either as a distribution for income or to convert to a Roth, his account was growing. When he reaches 70.5, he has to take out his required minimum distribution. This income is then taxable, as an IRA is money he did not pay taxes on when he contributed it, nor has it been taxed every year since.

This required distribution income will be so high in Jim's case, that it will cause 85% of his social security to become taxable. In contrast, right now, none of his social security income is taxable.

So, at 70.5, even though Jim neither wants nor needs the income from his IRA, he will be forced to take it out, and this will cause his taxes to go from $0 to approximately $7,000 a year. If his IRA continues to grow as he ages, his RMD will also grow, and consequently, so will his taxes.

Luckily for Jim, we have already developed a plan to convert enough of his IRA every year from now until 70.5 so that when the time comes, his RMD will not be large enough to cause his social security to be taxed and he can continue living in the elusive 0% tax bracket many of us desire, but believe is impossible to achieve.

So, have I convinced you that maybe the IRA is not the proper retirement savings vehicle? Great, so you are probably wondering what a good retirement savings vehicle is. I think it is The ROTH IRA!

This is one of those opportunities that I look at and say, "WOW, this is so good that one day soon it will either be changed or taken away, so get it while you can!!!"

The Roth IRA allows you to pay your taxes today on the money you put into it. Then, the money grows tax-free and when you take it out, you do not have to pay any more taxes on it. It is really that basic: pay now, not later.

As of the writing of this book, they don't even require you to take money out when you hit age 70.5, as with the traditional

IRA. This allows you to continue growing your money on a tax-free basis throughout your retirement.

This works especially well if you believe, as I do, that taxes may go up in the future. By paying your taxes today, you will protect your account from any possible future tax hikes. In addition to the Roth IRA, your company may offer a Roth 401(k). If they do, I typically recommend that you go that route.

There are a few exceptions; in my opinion if you are earning a significantly large amount of money, say $200-$400,000+, you may want to continue to use the traditional 401(k). Notice I did not say Roth IRA, because the government won't let you make pre-tax contributions to an IRA. You may be the exception and actually retire to a lower tax bracket.

Unless you have not only earned, but saved and invested well, then you may be like everyone else, stuck in the same, or worse, a higher bracket when taxes rise.

With all this said, I believe we need to know when to change back to paying our taxes as we save. As I said my opinion is that, in the 70s and early 80s, IRAs made sense. The same could hold true for the future, so that if taxes go up, you need to decide if you then could actually retire in a lower tax bracket. If the answer is "yes," then you may need to switch back from the Roth to the traditional IRA.

If this is all a bit confusing, I understand. This is why you should probably be looking for a qualified advisor to help. Refer back to the previous chapter where I discussed the different types of advisors available, and you may also want to visit www.WirbickResource.com to get more information on how taxes affect your retirement.

Let's get to back to George and Melinda. By now you may have guessed what George spent all that money on 15 years ago. If you guessed a Roth conversion, then you would be right. George took his 401k, moved it to an IRA, and then we converted it systematically to a Roth. The strategy with George is that we did not convert more money every year than what would place him in a higher tax bracket. Let's say that George's taxable income is $40,000. That puts him in the middle of the 15% tax bracket. If you want to know your own, get out your most recent tax return and look at line number 41. In George's case we knew that we could not convert more than around $30,000 a year because the top of the 15% bracket is in the mid $70,000s. To be safe, we would keep it less than that. So, every year George converted a portion of his IRA to a Roth.

This did cost George extra tax dollars every year that he did the conversion. I can also add that there were a few years that George was hesitant to shell out the extra tax dollars. Even his CPA thought he was making a mistake. Why would someone want to pay extra taxes? I think that is an easy question to answer if it means that they might live out their retirement completely income tax free!

It took a couple of years of converting before George's entire IRA was in his Roth. We knew that he would be still be contributing to his 401k for the next few years, but after some quick calculations, it appeared that the account would not grow to the point that the money he would be forced to take out at age 70.5 would cause him to pay any tax on his social security.

Now that George is retired and getting his social security checks, life is a bit easier without the worry of any federal income taxes. Because we live in Pennsylvania and they do not tax retirement income, George doesn't even have to pay state taxes. He can access his Roth IRA or his 401k without the fear of unknown future taxes. His accounts will also last him longer, because he only has to take out what he needs to spend, rather than having to remove excess money just to pay the taxes.

If George had not wanted a tax free retirement, and planned for it with my help and guidance, I think he would not be realizing the dream of a tax free life. This is just one example of how proper IRA planning could make a difference, not all may see the same results, however it is better to take a look at your scenario and begin planning today.

CHAPTER 4
I BELIEVE SOCIAL SECURITY IS TRUE SECURITY

The difference between death and taxes is death doesn't get worse every time Congress meets

~ Will Rogers ~

I was too old for a paper route, too young for Social Security, and too tired for an affair

~ Erma Bombeck ~

Security

Todd and Marie live up in New York. They love to sail on the Finger Lakes on the weekends, ski all winter long, and drink the many great wines of the region. They also wanted to retire some day and have enough income to continue to pursue all of their passions.

Marie is an executive at her company, and Todd is a freelance writer. Both have good incomes, and have enjoyed their careers. When we first met, they both were planning to take their social security incomes as soon as they were allowed. They thought that it was always better to get the money right away, and not delay the income. They are both very glad they took my advice and postponed that decision.

I honestly believe that social security is one of the most misunderstood retirement accounts that we have around today. You heard me correctly; I said retirement account. I am tired of people calling this an entitlement. This is money that you and I have invested throughout our entire working careers; it is not an entitlement!

Having said that, once you look at social security like your IRA or 401(k), it takes on a different meaning, and hopefully, you will treat it with the same reverence. Again, this is *your* money.

Unfortunately, I believe many people have not taken the time to understand the system and, therefore, they tend to make major, life-altering mistakes. If I told you that you stand to lose in excess of $500,000-$1,000,000 by choosing the wrong option, would that get your attention? Good, then let's start at the beginning.

Social Security was born out of the Great Depression, an era we will cover in more detail in Chapter 6. Franklin Delano Roosevelt was looking for a way to protect people in their retirement years. There had been many attempts to do this over the previous decade, and all had failed to follow through. On August 14, 1935, the Social Security Act was signed into law. In addition to several provisions for the general welfare, the new Act created a social insurance program designed to pay retired workers aged 65 or older a continuing income after retirement. Of course, as with all change, the Act was heralded as one that would eventually bankrupt the nation. Eighty years later, while we have considerably more debt, none of it was caused by Social Security. This is because you and I fund the system.

If you are currently working in the U.S., each time you get paid, the government removes 7.65% from your check to pay for Social Security and Medicare. This will occur until you make more than $118,000 (for the year 2015, this is indexed for inflation), at which time you will no longer be paying into Social Security. However, you will continue to have 1.45% deducted to fund Medicare.

For example, if you get out of college and begin your career at 22 making $50,000 a year, and achieve a 3% raise every year until age 65, you will have invested over $250,000 in the Social Security fund. That is a huge investment in my opinion. If you are like me, and started your own company at the age of 22, you will have invested over $500,000 in the system. The more you make, the more they take. I think this is a large amount of money, and you really should take a long, hard look at it and understand all the myriad options available to you.

Now, many of us have heard that the system is broke, but I don't think that is entirely correct. I believe the system is going broke. By the year 2033, if nothing changes, social security will only be able to pay out 77 cents on the dollar. You will notice that I said, if nothing changes. In fact, I think a few fixes will shore up the system indefinitely:

Option 1

If they were to increase the maximum earnings that are subject to social security from the current $118,000 (2015) to $250,000,

I think that would bring in enough extra revenue to cover the shortfall.

Option 2

If they were to raise the retirement age for people born after 1960 from 67 to age 70, I believe that would take care of any future shortfalls we can anticipate.

Option 3

They also could lower the future benefits for people born after 1960, which in my opinion could be one of the easiest fixes, because these people represent some of the lowest turnouts at the voting booth at election time.

Option 4

Alternatively, they could reduce or eliminate everyone's cost of living adjustments (COLAs). I see this as the most difficult option, as it would affect current retirees, and they have the world's largest lobby, the American Association of Retired People (AARP). I think this would work, but good luck getting re-elected.

As you can see, there are many options available to fix the system, and although I am not sure which one, or how many they will use, in my opinion it will be fixed. However, I would not want to be the politician responsible for killing Social Security. I don't think you would even be able to get elected dogcatcher in your own neighborhood if you did that.

Now, let's explore how Social Security works and how you can potentially get the most out of it.

Individual Benefits

First, simply put, the more you earn and the longer you work, the more you get. If you were born between 1943-1954, your full retirement age (the age at which your benefit will not be reduced) is 66. If you were born between 1954-1960, then your retirement age will fall between 66-67, and if you were born after 1960, then it is age 67.

The next thing you probably want to do is to get a copy of your personal Social Security statement. The Social Security department used to mail these out to everyone who contributes. However, due to funding issues, and the high cost of printing and mailing, this practice ended many years ago. When it ceased, many people may have forgotten about it, and never bothered to look into their benefit further.

Think about it; if the government thought it was important for you to see your statement, there must be a reason. Actually, I think there are a few.

Reason One

You should make sure that the department has been recording your income data correctly since you began contributing. This is your responsibility, and is one that you should take very seriously. If they have not been recording your income as you have been making it, it is your fault. You read that right. If they put the wrong numbers into the system, you are the one to blame. Not only is it your responsibility, but you can also only go back 7 years to make corrections. Can you see how important it is to check your statement?

Reason Two

You should start to get an idea of how much (or how little) you will be receiving. This is only their best guess, but you should consider it in your overall retirement picture.

One easy way to get your current statement is to check out the link for the free resource at www.WirbickResource.com. On there you can create your own account, login, and print out a copy of your statement. I recommend checking the accuracy of the numbers annually. If there are mistakes, get down to your local Social Security office immediately.

Okay, so now we know when we can retire, and that the more we made and the longer we worked, the more we get. What's next? Let's focus on your own benefits and then we can move on to the spousal option.

You have probably heard of people collecting Social Security before the age of 65, which is an option. However, in my opinion *it is a very expensive option.* If you choose to collect early, it may reduce your benefit by 25%. For example, if your age 66 full retirement benefit would be $2,000 (this is known as your Primary Insurance Amount, which we will refer to as a PIA from this point on). If you choose to retire at 62, you would only receive $1,500. Once you take the reduced benefit, you cannot get a higher one as you age, except for the COLAs. Unfortunately, today, almost half of all people claim their benefits early, I believe it is at age 62. This may be the worst financial option out there.

Let's take someone who is supposed to receive a PIA of $2,000 a month at age 66, as we just discussed, but they decide to take early retirement. That individual will lose over $100,000 in payments if they live to an average life expectancy. I am not ready to just give up $100,000, are you?

But wait, there's more. While the system penalizes you if you take the benefit early, they reward you if you take it later. There is a guaranteed 8% increase in your benefit for every year you wait past the age of 66 (or your full retirement age), to a maximum of age 70. This is known as a delayed credit. I don't know about you, but I don't know where I can get a guaranteed 8% growth on my money, and I do this stuff for a living. In my book this is not a small pile of cash. I have estimated that I will pay in over $400,000 into social security over my lifetime; I would love to know that I can get a future 8% guarantee on that money. That gets me excited.

So, with the same example we used before, a person with a PIA of $2,000 a month at retirement chooses to retire early and loses over $100,000. Let's change it up. What if we compare retiring early to deferring it as long as they let us? Are you ready for this number? Over $700,000 of lost income! I, for one, am not up to giving the government that kind of money, no sir. I want to get as much as I possibly can.

You can see now from the hypothetical examples provided starting too early can be dangerous, and deferring it can be beneficial. So, let's take a look at other benefits you may receive from Social Security.

Spousal Benefits

Because Social Security began during an age when single earner households were common, there has always been a benefit for the partner who earns less. They designed it so that the spouse who earns less has the ability, at full retirement age, to take half of the benefit of the spouse whose earnings are higher.

Let's say that John and Susan are married. John's PIA is $2,000, but Susan stayed home to raise the kids, and has only done some part-time work, so that her PIA is only $500. Susan does not need to retire and only collect $500, because if she waits until the full retirement age of 66, and John also has reached his full retirement age, she will get 50% of Johns' PIA, or $1,000! Unless s/he requests it specifically, the spouse who earns less will basically receive his/her own benefit and then the extra will be covered by the higher earner's PIA. This payout to his wife will not affect John's future income. Now the key to making this work is that John will need to file for Social Security before Susan can collect her spousal benefit. We will cover later how John can file so his wife gets her benefit, and he still receives his delayed credit of 8%. You can see that even though Susan did not earn enough to receive a benefit of $1,000, her spousal benefit allows her to get more money for the rest of her life.

Let's say that Susan's PIA was closer to $900 a month. She will still want to collect half of her husband's benefit, but she will ask to have a "restricted spousal benefit." This will give her only half of his PIA and allow her own to continue earning the 8% delayed credit up to age 70. Upon reaching 70, with the delayed credits and COLA, her benefit may have increased substantially to over $1,300 a month. She can now go back to her Social Security office and ask to receive her own benefit.

If the spouse decided to retire early, of course s/he will receive less than the full 50% benefit, just like when you choose to receive your own benefit before full retirement age.

All of these options are completely legitimate. However, the staff at the Social Security office cannot help you select any of the most advanced options. They can only calculate your own PIA. So, don't go there and start asking about which would be better, taking your own or your spouse's, because they cannot answer those questions.

Divorced Spousal Benefits

Did you know that if you were married to someone for more than 10 years and then divorced, you may be entitled to divorced spousal benefits? The benefits amount is the same as if you were married. You must attain age 62, not have remarried, and if the divorce was more than two years ago, your ex does not have to have filed for his/her own benefits. The ex is never notified that this is occurring; in fact, you don't even need to know where s/he is living. You just need to have your marriage license, and divorce decree, and head down to your local Social Security office and ask to file for divorced spousal benefits. Just like spousal benefits, the earlier you apply, the less you get. You can file a restricted spousal benefit at full retirement age to allow your own PIA to accumulate delayed credits until age 70.

Let's go back to Susan and John. Like many married couples in the U.S. today, let's assume they've been married for ten years, and decide to get a divorce. Susan still has a PIA of only $900, but, as in our example above, she can elect all of the same, different scenarios as if they were still married. The difference is, if the divorce occurred more than two years ago, Susan does not have to wait for John to file for his own benefit in order to collect her spousal benefit.

Now, imagine that John goes out and gets married again; it lasts ten years, and he gets divorced again. He decides the third time's a charm and gets married one last time, but unfortunately, at the ten-year mark, his new spouse gets sick of him and walks out. Did you know that all three of these ex-spouses can file for, and receive, full spousal benefits from John, without affecting him or any of the other two ladies?

Are you starting to see why Social Security has a funding shortage? I think these benefits were designed for a different age, when marriages lasted longer, and no one could foresee the future, and how it would affect social security's coffers. You can read further on this at www.WirbickResource.com.

Survivor Benefits

If you are married to someone for at least nine months and s/he passes away, you also are entitled to spousal benefits. In this case, you can choose to have your widow's benefit paid out as early as age 60. Of course, however, this will reduce your benefit significantly, now and in the future.

In my opinion the best way to maximize your annual income may be to wait until full retirement, take your spouse's benefit, and then allow yours to grow and take it at age 70. You will want to consult a professional to help you calculate this and to obtain further recommendations.

If you both were taking your social security benefits at the time your spouse passed, you might switch to his/her benefit if it is higher than your own. If you do this, you should stop receiving your benefit and begin receiving that of the deceased spouse.

Unless you remarry after the age of 60, if you are receiving your survivor benefit and decide to remarry, the income will stop.

John and Susan now are both retired and receiving their full PIAs; John is getting his $2,000 a month, and Susan is receiving her spousal benefit of $1,000. If John were to pass, Susan could stop getting her spousal benefit of $1,000 and start getting John's full benefit of $2,000 a month. Unfortunately, that means her total income would be reduced by $1,000 a month. This may make things difficult for Susan if she and John have not done prior planning to account for this decrease in income.

I routinely say this is exactly why I want the spouse who has the highest PIA to defer his/her income until 70 if possible in order to ensure a higher survivor benefit, especially if the higher earning spouse is male, as we tend to die first. Although that has begun to change slightly over the last few years, the average woman still will outlive her husband by 7 years!

Did you know the average age of a widow in America today is only 56? If Susan had become a widow at age 56, she would be unable to access either her own or John's benefit. She could be in trouble, as she does not have a high-paying, full-time career to rely on, and those four years until she is able to collect a widow's benefit could be a very long, hard four years.

Claim Some Now, Get More Later

This next benefit I am going to discuss is only available until 2019. Why? I find that whenever the Government takes away benefits, you can be sure it's because that benefit was really good for us, and not so good for them!

Let's go back to John and Susan again for the next example. Assume that John's PIA is $2,000 still and Susan's is $800.

They, of course, could just apply for their individual incomes and be done with it. However, that could cost them hundreds of thousands of dollars.

In this scenario, I recommend to have them both defer their benefits until full retirement age. Then, I would have Susan file for her own benefit and John file for spousal benefits. Wait, you might be thinking, why in the world would John apply for spousal benefits if his own are so much higher. Let's take a look at both scenarios.

John files and suspends at age 66 = $0

Susan apples for spousal benefit at 66 = $1,000

Total is $1,000

Susan applies for her own benefit at 66 = $800

John applies for his spousal benefit at 66 = $400

The total is now *$1,200*, which is $200 more a month for the next four years; this quick math means they will receive an additional $9,600, without taking COLAs into account.

Now, when John applies, he needs to be sure to request to have a restricted spousal benefit, because in that way, he will get half of Susan's and continue to receive his delayed credits of 8% until age 70. Then, when they reach age 70, the picture changes to this.

John age 70 = $2,640

Susan age 70 = $1,000

Total is $3,640 without taking COLAs into account.

This is the same total as our last scenario. However, the couple received more money from age 66-70, which did not hurt them in the long run.

As you can see, these are just a few of the many scenarios you can construct for your own retirement. Have fun with it, see a professional, and have them run the numbers for you. Don't put this off; start early, and then check back in often to see how the numbers look. Unfortunately, these will all be best guesses. The numbers that social security reports to you are not definite and can change over time. However, these are a great place to start, and then you can see what other planning you need to do to enjoy a successful retirement.

The Aged Parent College Fund

This is my favorite, and I think the least publicly known benefit available through the Social Security department. If you wish to learn a lot more about social security, you can visit www.WirbickResource.com and I have some great resources for you.

If you are the parent of a child under the age of 18 and you are at your full retirement age, then that child is eligible to receive 50% of your PIA!

Let's go back to John and Susan. Let's say they have a son, Jim, who is 16. John has just turned 66, so he is eligible for social security, and so is Jim. If John files for his benefit and his PIA is $2,000, then Jim could receive $1,000 a month until he turns 18. The social security department wants this money to go towards Jim's expenses, such as college. What a great way to pay for Jim's college.

Just like a spousal benefit, this will not preclude Susan from also collecting her own spousal benefit if she so desires.

Now that you know more about the benefits offered by social security, let's take a look at how the benefit could affect your overall retirement picture.

Taxes on Social Security

When social security began, the government promised that we would never have to pay taxes on the benefits we receive in retirement. That lasted until 1983, when they said that only up to 50% of social security income could be taxed. That ruling held for 10 more years, until 1993, when 85% of our benefit could become taxable.

Here's how it works. If you are married, filing jointly, and make less than $32,000 of earned income, dividends, and interest (even from tax-free bonds), and half of your social security income, then you pay no tax on your social security income. For individual filers, the initial threshold is $25,000.

If you are filing jointly, and the income above exceeds $32,000, but does not exceed $44,000, then 50% of your benefit is taxable. For individual filers, the limits are $25,000-$34,000.

If you file jointly, and your above-stated income exceeds $44,000, then 85% of your social security benefit becomes taxable. For individual filers, it must exceed $34,000.

I think this is a very important point to understand, because people often overlook it, and it can end up costing them thousands of extra tax dollars every year of their retirement. Let's look at an example.

Frank has a pretty simple retirement. He has a pension that pays him $1,000 a month, his social security is $2,000 a month, and he has tax-free municipal bonds that return $1,000 a month interest. He understands that the interest from his bonds are tax-exempt, but what he fails to recognize is that they are used to calculate that tax on his social security income.

Pension = $12,000

Bond Interest = $12,000

Social Security = $12,000 (only 50% is used to calculate tax)

Total = $36,000

If Frank is single, then 85% of his $24,000 social security, or $20,400 would now be taxable. That puts him into the 15% tax bracket; actually, it almost pushes him into the 25% bracket, all because he is withdrawing from his taxable investments.

Once Frank hits 70.5 and starts taking his RMDs, this could add thousands of additional tax dollars to his bottom line.

This is why I do not believe social security planning is an island. What I mean is that you should consider it together with all of your other retirement accounts, and figure it into your overall plan in order to maximize the net dollars you receive.

If Frank were to convert his IRAs to Roths before attaining age 70.5, and move his investment dollars from "tax-free" Municipal Bonds to true tax-free strategy, then none of his social security would be taxable, possibly for the rest of his life.

Let's get back to Todd and Marie sailing around the Finger Lakes. As I said, they both were planning to take Social Security at the full retirement age and not take advantage of the delayed credits or any of the spousal planning techniques available.

I ran six different scenarios for them and they decided that it was best for Marie to file at age 69, when she is ready to retire, and let Todd take his spousal benefit when he reached age 66. This gave them extra income they never knew they could receive and because Todd is still working, they could invest in their retirement funds.

When both Todd and Marie reach age 70, their combined social security income will be in excess of $80,000 a year! Not too bad. Neither one of them ever imagined that they could receive such a significant portion of their retirement income from social security. Now all they have to do is figure out when they want to stop working and start their dream retirement.

I care about our young people, and I wish them great success, because they are our Hope for the Future, and some day, when my generation retires, they will have to pay us trillions of dollars in social security

~ Dave Barry ~

I found a way for my social security check to cover my bills; I stack my bills up all nice and neat, and then lay my social security check on top

~ Author Unknown ~

CHAPTER 5
THAT'S LIFE (INSURANCE)

The best life insurance policy you can own is one that is still in place on the day you die

~ Joe Wirbick ~

John is a healthy, 35-year-old executive living the good life in Southern Florida with his beautiful wife, Sarah, and their two young children, Melissa and Mark. John makes a very nice living and his wife stays at home with the kids. Even though John is doing well financially, he and Sarah enjoy the finer things life has to offer and tend to spend all of John's paycheck each month.

He does contribute to his company's 401(k) and has managed to save over $150,000 since he started. When approached by his financial planner about adding extra life insurance to his portfolio, John replied that he was covered adequately at work and frankly, he didn't have the extra money in his budget. Unfortunately, his planner did not do a good enough job showing John the shortfalls in his insurance coverage and John truly believed that, between his company's two times his salary life insurance, and his 401(k) balance, his family would be covered. And really, John was an active, healthy 35-year-old, so he felt invincible.

Had John looked into it further, he could have purchased an additional $1,000,000 of term insurance for a monthly premium amount less than what he spent monthly at Starbucks.

John was playing Frisbee with his son, Mark, at the pool one sunny day and he slipped while attempting to catch one of Mark's wicked tosses. John landed on his side and was pretty banged up, but it was nothing serious. He walked away a little sore, but more embarrassed.

What John didn't know was that he was born with a small blood clot in his stomach. Although it was fine for the first 35 years, his fall at the pool dislodged the clot and it began making its deadly trek to his brain.

The next morning, while enjoying breakfast with his family, John suddenly got woozy, stood up at the table, and fell over dead, leaving Sarah, Melissa, and Mark without a loving husband and caring Father.

Unfortunately, John was wrong about having adequate coverage. His wife had to cash in his 401(k) at a tax cost of over $50,000, leaving her with around $300,000 of cash between it and John's life insurance payout.

If she invested it, it would barely make Sarah $15-20,000 a year in income, far short of the six figures John had made. Sarah was forced to sell the family home at a loss, move to a different part of town, and take on a full-time job. Now Melissa and Mark have no father, and only get to see their mother when she isn't working.

Had John purchased a more appropriate amount of coverage, he could have secured their future, kept them in their home, and allowed Sarah to continue to raise her children as she was before his death.

Buying life insurance is one of the single most important decisions you will ever make in my opinion. Do not take this lightly, and do not put this off.

Having spent the past 20 years working with many different companies, other advisors, and with many clients, the one thing I can say for certain about life insurance is that just about everyone has their own opinion about it.

I hear all kinds of very good and very nasty reports about life insurance. People will tell me it costs too much, it makes the insurance agent a big commission, I don't need any life insurance, it is a horrible investment, and on and on.

Here is what I have to say about life insurance: I feel it is like any good prescription medication. If a competent doctor recommends it, and a person takes it as prescribed, it can do amazing things. The same is true of life insurance. If a competent advisor recommends it, and it is used correctly, it can transform people's financial lives, and help them and their heirs for generations to come.

The problem is that not only do customers misunderstand life insurance, but often the agent selling the policy does as well. I have seen countless examples over the years in which an agent sold a client a policy that was not the right fit for him/her.

I am here to dispel many of the myths about life insurance, let you in on the insider secrets about the policies, and help you understand better what it can do, not only for the loved ones you leave behind, but equally importantly, what it may do for you and your retirement portfolio.

Insurance 101

There are three main types of life insurance on the market today. I am going to go over each of them and address their pros and cons. They are:

Term Life
Whole Life
Universal Life

Now, there are dozens of subcategories of each of these types, but for the purposes of our discussion, we are going to focus only on the major policies out there today.

Term Life

Let's start with what I believe is the most basic policy issued today, Term. It is very easy to understand, because it is life insurance in its purest form. There is no cash value to worry about, only a stated death benefit, and a stated period: that's it.

It is usually the cheapest of all life insurance because all of your premium dollars are going to the insurance company. This will cover the cost of the policy should you die during the term you purchased. Most often it is offered in 10-year increments up to 30 years.

Be careful here, because some policies will guarantee level premiums during the term, while others will not, so make sure you know what you are buying.

The reason they call it Term insurance is that you should only be buying this for a particular term or period. The insurance company will underwrite you for that period, and then they want you to go away. Let me give you an example:

John is a healthy, 40-year-old and he needs $1 million of term insurance to protect his young family. He shops around (as you should; Term is really a commodity. I recommend you go with the company that offers the lowest price and has the highest ratings) and finds a policy that costs him around $1,400 a year, which in my opinion is a very affordable way to buy large amounts of life insurance. However, if John still needs that coverage in year 21, his premium jumps from $1,400 to an incredible $18,000! That is an increase of 1,285%. Why? We call this adverse selection. The company no longer wishes to insure John, because his risk of dying has increased exponentially, and they did not underwrite him beyond the 20 years.

What happens if John still needs coverage? Will he be able to get more Term insurance from another carrier at 60? Maybe, if his health has not deteriorated. However, it is going to cost quite a lot more than what he was paying. According to hypothetical scenarios run in 2015, it would cost a 60-year-old $10,000 a year, quite a bit more than the $1,400 he was paying at age 40.

Want to know a rare fact about Term insurance? Less than 2% of Term policies ever pay out a death claim. That means that 98% of the people who pay for them are just giving their hard-earned money to the insurance industry.

Let's look at John again. We could ask him this question. John, would you be willing to bet $28,000 of your money ($1,400 a year for 20 years) on a $1,000,000 payoff if you knew you had a 98% chance of losing? I have asked many of my clients this question, and the majority of them have answered "No!" I am not saying that Term is bad; I am just trying to get you to understand when it may be right for you.

What is the moral of the story when it comes to Term? In my professional opinion, it works for younger people who may not be able to afford more permanent coverage, or for people who are really just trying to insure themselves for a certain period.

Personally, I carry $5,000,000 of 20-year Term. I do this for two reasons: first, it is affordable in my budget. Second, I still have young kids and a wife who would need a large influx of cash should I pass suddenly. I have asked myself the gambling question above, and answered "yes," I would place that bet.

What you don't know is that I also carry permanent insurance, which we will cover next.

So, if you are uncertain whether you have enough insurance, or whether Term is right for you, then contact me for a free consultation. Additionally, you can find out more at www.WirbickResource.com.

Whole Life

You might consider whole life is sort of the grandfather of life insurance. This type of policy has been around the longest, and is probably what you think of when you think of life insurance.

The reason it is called "whole life" is that if you pay your premiums, then the policy will be there for the rest of your life. This type definitely meets my definition of the best type of policy to have, as it will be there on the day you die.

I do have some reservations about whole life insurance. The cost is my biggest concern. Most whole life policies guarantee two things:

Death benefit
Cash Value

Unlike Term insurance, where your premium simply covers the cost of insurance, whole life premiums are significantly higher because the company must also guarantee the cash value.

As the company has so much risk on its plate, it needs to bring in higher premium dollars to make the policy work. This extra cost will reduce the amount of cash value you actually have left over. What happens eventually is that the cash value is guaranteed to grow to equal the death benefit. At this point, the policy becomes what is known as an endowment, and is no longer classified as life insurance.

Typically, policies won't reach this point, because people either cash them in early or die before the endowment date. If you do hold the policy until endowment, it now becomes cash and no longer is a death benefit. You can spend the money or leave it in the policy; however, when inherited, the growth on the cash after endowment will be taxable to your beneficiaries.

You can see that buying a whole life insurance policy will give you cash and a death benefit. This means you will always have some money in the policy should you wish to cancel it, unlike a Term policy, where you get no money back when you cancel it.

Universal Life

Universal life is an interesting policy. It can be tweaked to behave like a Term policy or more like a whole life policy. You can ask the insurance company only to guarantee the death benefit and not keep any extra cash in it. This will reduce the cost of the insurance, although it will not be as low as term. However, you can have the guarantee extended all the way out to 120! Not sure who will live that long, but peace of mind is important to some.

You can also tweak the policy to have higher or lower cash values depending on your needs. Maybe you are looking for a smaller death benefit, but you would also like a place to grow some extra savings. You can design a policy that will behave more like an annuity, in that the cash value will grow, tax-deferred, and the death benefit will start at a much lower level, which will mean lower costs and a higher return in cash potential.

Or, you can follow the guidelines of the tax code, section 7702, which says that you can pay in premiums with a higher death benefit and allow your cash value to grow at a tax-favored rate, which allows you to withdraw money in the future on a tax-free basis.

You can also choose to have your money put into a variable or a fixed universal life contract. A variable contract grows based on market returns and a fixed contract is based either on the company's internal returns or on fixed index returns.

As you can see, universal life insurance offers a broad range of options, and can be tailored individually. These policies can just provide lifetime death benefits protection, or be more advanced, and add in possible tax-free cash value for future income. The possibilities truly are endless.

I believe this is definitely an occasion when you need a professional to help you decide what is right for you and your family.

CHAPTER 6
I BELIEVE YOUR HOME IS NOT YOUR BANK

The one thing that offends me the most is when I walk by a bank and see ads trying to convince people to take out second mortgages on their home so they can go on vacation. That's approaching evil

~ Jeff Bezos ~

Your home, house, humble abode—there are many terms that describe the building in which you reside. Over the years, many have moved from farms in the 1800s to cities in the early 1900s. The early 30s saw a large migration to single-family homes, and by the 50s, a house with a white picket fence was becoming more common, and suburban areas appeared overnight all over this great nation of ours.

Now it appears that the next generation may be moving back to the city and we could see suburbia disappear in the rear-view mirror.

Wherever it is we decide to live, it is likely to be the single largest investment most of us will ever make. Using the majority of our paychecks each month to cover the mortgage is the common. However, throughout the years, many have been tempted to buy more than maybe we can handle, or, to pull out more money from the home than it is actually worth.

There are countless theories out there about home ownership. Most say it is better than renting, some say it is a better investment than any that the stock market has to offer, and many believe that while others have seen their homes fall in value, theirs will rise forever and one day be worth significantly more than they ever paid for it, thereby allowing them to retire on its ever-flowing amounts of cash.

Let's take a look at how houses have been bought throughout the last century, and try to learn from history rather than be forced to repeat it.

In the early 1900s, banks were not willing to offer today's gold standard 30-year mortgage. In fact, the norm back then was a scant 5-year note. Now, you weren't forced to pay the house off in 5 years; you were only guaranteed that they would not call the loan until 5 years had expired. Typically, at the end of the 5 years, the bank would float you another 5-year note, and so on and so forth until the home was paid off.

Another popular trend at the same time was withdrawing your home value through a loan, and investing all the money in the ever-increasing stock market with which the country was blessed during the "Roaring 20s."

Unfortunately, what we know happened to that market in the early 30s was unknown to our predecessors, and when the stock market crashed in 1932 many people lost all the money they had invested. That money was not theirs, so the problem was compounded greatly. In fact, over 80% of the money invested at the time was on margin or loaned out from people's homes.

For many people when the bank loans were called at the end of the 5-year notes, the market had not recovered, in fact did not recover fully until 1951, so many people did not have the money to cover their notes, and, as a result, the banks made mass repossessions of houses nationwide. This was another factor in the Great Depression, and a driving force in creating the 30-year mortgage we know today.

Because all of this occurred before many of us were born, and we aren't all students of financial history, we saw a similar housing financial crisis strike us in 2008.

In the early 2000s, the stock market lost a considerable amount of money and investors were looking for safe places to put their money. Banks began to offer bundled mortgages as a low risk source of high possible returns, and the world began to invest in very large sums. Soon, banks did not have mortgages to offer, so they began the creative process of offering riskier financial products never before, and hopefully, never again, seen.

Products like the NINJA loan, which meant "No Income, No Jobs, No Assets." It's unimaginable, but true: banks were offering people with no income, no jobs, no assets whatsoever, multimillion dollar loans, just so they could bundle them and sell them at profit to foreign investors, and large insurance companies who needed "safe" investments in their books.

Most people can see where this is headed, and sure enough, 2008 came, the market began to unravel, and it became clear that the houses the banks thought would always go up in value, were suddenly losing value at a pace that seemed faster than the Titanic sank into the frigid waters of the Atlantic many years ago.

Again, we saw mass foreclosures, as banks repossessed the same houses on which they were so quick to offer unreasonable amounts of money. The federal government stepped in, and bailed out the banks and the insurance companies that had bought many of the worthless mortgages.

What can we learn from all this? First in my opinion, your home is not your bank; you should not refinance it repeatedly; you should not withdraw from it all of the value that it has gained over the years you have owned it. This is your house, your home, the place that keeps your family safe. It is not to be trifled with.

We also have to ask ourselves if home ownership is truly a good investment. That is a difficult question to answer, because geographical location is a significant factor in the future value of your house. In addition, demographics will play a large part in what your home will be worth in the future.

Let's explore what I think is best way to buy a home. We'll use two twin brothers who want to own a home. We will call them Brother A and Brother B; their parents were not very original. Both brothers want to purchase a $300,000 home and use a 30-year mortgage at 6%.

Brother A is a very conservative individual who believes debt is bad. Therefore, he has saved for many years and gives the bank a 20% deposit on his home ($60,000 out of his pocket). He then decides to make double payments because he wants to pay off the loan as fast as possible. So, A is not paying the $1,500 a month he is required to, he is instead doubling up and paying $3,000 a month in mortgage payments.

Brother B has saved the same $60,000, but he is none too keen to sink all of his available cash into a house that he is not sure will always grow in value. He finds a bank that only requires 5% down (a mere $15,000) and invests the remaining $45,000 into a blend of investments that yield him 6% a year. B also is not afraid of debt, and so is not in a hurry to pay off his loan; thus, he only pays the minimum the bank requires, $1,700 a month. Then, and this is very *important*, he makes monthly investments of the extra that $1,300 his Brother A was giving to the bank into the same account in which he deposited the $45,000.

Now A is giving all his money to the bank in an attempt to pay the loan off as fast as possible, because he still believes debt is bad, while in contrast, B is attempting to grow his cash on a monthly basis, planning that he will have sufficient money should something bad happen.

Let's fast forward 5 years. A has been making double payments this whole time and has managed to lower his mortgage all the way down to $118,675 while B still owes a whopping $264,822. However, B's savings have grown to an impressive $148,158. As a reminder this is a hypothetical example and is assuming a static non-variable annualized investment return to emphasis the illustration. However, all investments contain risks including possible loss of principal.

Let's pause here for a second and look at the two brothers' finances. Which one appears to be in a better position? Some of you may say Brother A, because he has less debt, while others would argue Brother B, because he has more cash. Let's continue and see what happens.

Unfortunately, the economy grows weak, and both brothers lose their jobs. Brother A is unable to afford his monthly mortgage payment. He heads down to the bank and requests a few months off due to his history of making double payments. What do you think the bank says? NO! Of course not; extra payments do not, in my opinion compensate for future ones.

Brother B does not bother going to the bank, because he has $148,158. He can easily make the monthly payments by simply removing them from his savings.

Let's take a look at how the bank now views these two mortgages: assume they wished to foreclose on one of them. Brother A now owes only $118,675 on a house worth $300,000. Brother B still owes $264,822 on his. Which house do you think is more attractive to the bank in a foreclosure situation? Brother A's house, of course: you see, the bank can stand to sell his house at a value significantly lower than market value and still come out ahead. However, Brother B's house may be more difficult to sell because its mortgage value is so close to its market value.

This scenario only works if Brother B puts the down payment money into an account and continues to put the extra money he would have spent on the mortgage into the same account. If he decided to use the down payment money on a sports car and the extra payments each month on vacations and food, he would be in the same situation his brother is in, with no money to continue to pay the mortgage if he lost his job.

You need to have discipline to make this work.

So, we can see that debt is not always bad. I believe that debt can get you very far in life. Many wealthy people I know use debt to their own advantage. Again, this is one example of how using "other people's money" to get ahead financially. Therefore, you must analyze each situation carefully and make sure it is a sound investment.

I do not think that all debt is good: credit card debt is usually unwise, as they tend to charge high interest rates, and you probably won't be making too much off your credit card purchases. Therefore, you have to be very selective.

As I mentioned earlier, cash is, and I believe always will be, king. When you hold the cash, you make the rules. Moreover, I think the best time to ask for more access to cash is when you don't need it. Get pre-approved. Hold onto lines of credit. Only use them when absolutely necessary, in emergency situations, because in emergencies, banks tend to look the other way.

Reverse Mortgages

Jim and Cara Miller own their home outright, meaning they have no debt on it. It is in a small, rural area of the country and it appears that none of their adult children have any interest in living in the house once mom and dad are gone.

The Miller's home is worth $650,000. They have always wanted a vacation home near the beach, but now they have retired and are living on a fixed income—a comfortable one due to their investments and Cara's pension—but a fixed income nonetheless.

Cara hears about a reverse mortgage and asks Jim if he knows anything about them. Jim has heard rumors, but doesn't understand fully how they work. Jim decides to ask their liscensed mortgage professional, Steve.

Steve meets with the Millers and explains how a reverse mortgage works. He tells them that the Federal Government now oversees these loans and has strict guidelines with respect to how banks may offer them. He also informs them that they can borrow up to 80% of their home's value, or $520,000.

This will be tax-free money that they can leave as a line of credit or draw on in its entirety whenever they wish. However, they can choose to sell the house whenever they desire, and pay off the loan from the proceeds.

When it comes time to sell the home, after both Jim and Cara have passed, or after they have decided to sell, the bank may only take enough money to pay off the original loan, plus loan origination fees, and all the interest the loan has accumulated over the years.

There are three scenarios that Steve presents to the Millers.

Scenario 1

The Miller's home has increased significantly in value and exceeded that of the loan. At that time, the bank recaptures its money, and the excess goes to either Jim or Cara if they are living, or to their estate if they have passed.

Scenario 2

The Miller's house has kept pace with interest and sells for the exact value of the reverse mortgage. In this case, the bank keeps all the money, and the estate gets no additional value from the sale of the home.

Scenario 3

The Miller's house has not done well, and the value has not kept up with the interest on the loan. When the house sells, which it must if they die, the bank may only capture what the house sells for in a fair market. If this does not cover the cost of the loan, the bank takes the loss only when the homeowners are deceased. The Miller's estate is not liable for any extra money.

Jim and Cara love the idea and think that using the value of their home to purchase another house is a wise decision. Cara then asks the question, "Are there any payments that have to be made towards the reverse mortgage during the period of the loan?"

"Excellent question," Steve says. "No, Cara, there are never any payments that need to be made. This is not a home equity loan that needs to be repaid. The money is yours to spend and the bank only wants it paid back should you decide to sell while you're alive, or your estate sells the house once you both have passed."

Cara and Jim decide to move ahead with the reverse mortgage. Steve recommends some local banks they can deal with in order to process the loan. He recommends that they only use the money for another home purchase, or if they need the extra monthly income to meet their basic daily needs. He tells them that they should not use the money to invest in any type of security, annuity, or life insurance product.

Jim and Cara head to the beach to buy their dream vacation home. Their kids and grandkids love visiting, and now are definitely interested in having this new property passed on to them. You see, their main home will have a debt on it for life, but the beach house was paid for in cash, which ensures that it will be unencumbered when they both pass.

You can see that a reverse mortgage may benefit you if you meet the criteria we saw in the story above. It definitely benefitted Jim and Cara. If you feel that it could benefit you also, then contact your licensed mortgage professional and explore this option together. It is important to note that reverse mortgages are complex lending agreements and often have higher fees and interest rates than traditional loans. Conditions resulting in immediate repayment or foreclosure proceedings should be reviewed carefully as they can be initiated by the lender while the homeowner is alive and experiencing a medical event, causing the homeowner to be moved into a medical care facility even on a short-term basis. Certain government programs such as Medicaid, which are based upon liquid assets may be negatively impacted by reverse mortgages and eligibility may be last. Eviction may occur if all homeowners are not also listed on the reverse mortgage contract. Due to these perils it is imperative that homeowners carefully review the loan and discussions with mortgage professionals and heirs is strongly recommended.

It is good to have an end to journey toward; but it is the journey that matters, in the end
~ Ernest Hemingway ~

CHAPTER 7
WHY WAIT?

I try to treat each evening and weekend as little slices of retirement because no one is guaranteed a lengthy one at the end of their career

~ Mike Hamma ~

When I was in high school, I worked in many different industries, but my favorite was the restaurant world. I found I had a way with people. They seemed to like me immediately.

One evening while I was working at my hometown's best steakhouse, a man was having his retirement dinner; let's call him Sam. All of Sam's friends and coworkers were there. He had spent the last 45 years working for an unnamed company, giving them his life, and now he was about to retire. He was going to be able to set his own schedule, be his own boss, travel the world, spend more time with his wife, kids, and grandkids—in short, do all those things he spent the last 45 years dreaming about.

I could see his friends were happy for him, maybe even a little jealous that they would not be retiring, but happy nonetheless. People were talking excitedly, drinks were flowing, and there was much laughter. After the meal, the wait staff brought out a big cake to much applause and fanfare. I can still see it now: "Happy Retirement," in blue and green icing. They rolled it out on a dolly and everyone sang, "For he's a jolly good fellow." I'm not kidding; they actually sang that song to him. It was like something out of a movie.

Then it all went horribly wrong. After the song, people shouted a rousing "Speech, speech," from all corners of the room, and Sam stood to much applause and approached the front of the room. He raised his glass, and was about to speak when he suddenly clutched his chest and dropped over dead. He died right there, at his own retirement party, in front of all his loved ones. It was still like something out of a movie, but now a very dark, disturbing movie. People were frantic. They could not believe what had happened.

They called the ambulance, covered Sam with a blanket, and wheeled him out on a stretcher. I remember seeing the panicked looks on the faces of the other diners in the restaurant.

I know that was another defining moment in my life. I was able to see firsthand, and at a very young age, that you can't always put off your dreams for another day. I believe this is why I've always wanted to live a "working retirement."

What does that mean, a "working retirement?" It means I'm not waiting until I'm 65 or 70 to start doing all those things people typically put off until retirement. I have spent the last twenty years seeing personally that you are not always your healthiest when you reach your 60s—shocking, I know.

I decided that while I worked smart and hard, I would take plenty of time off to enjoy life's many pleasures. I actually believe it is this time off that has led to my many successes in life.

Craig and Laura are clients of mine who epitomize the idea of a working retirement. Craig is a middle school history teacher, and Laura teaches high school economics. Both have a desire to live life to the fullest. Craig grew up in Seattle and spent his childhood summers sailing the Sound. Laura never sailed, but Craig's enthusiasm rubbed off on her, and soon she found herself loving the ocean and the wind as much as Craig did. Because their jobs gave them the summers off, both realized early on that they wanted to spend that time relaxing, exploring, and rejuvenating their souls. However, two teachers' salaries were not sufficient to fund a three-month long vacation.

Craig and Laura had to think outside of the box. With Craig's knowledge of sailing and Laura's business acumen, they soon developed a plan. They would save up enough money over the next few years to buy a sailboat. However, sailing the same old waterways that Craig grew up on did not excite either of them enough to sacrifice vacations for a few years. They both dreamed of island hopping in Greece. The Mediterranean sounded a lot more exciting. Imagine, summers spent overseas. That would be a dream come true.

But how would they transport a boat overseas and then bring it back every summer? They thought about storing it in Greece, but the costs were prohibitive.

Then Laura came up with the idea of a lifetime. They would not buy the boat in America. Instead, they would purchase one in Greece, thereby saving themselves time and money in transporting the boat overseas. Rather than storing the boat, she decided they could sell it at the end of the summer, pocket the money, and use it to purchase another boat the next year.

Problem solved! Not only would they not have to worry about storing or shipping fees, they could enjoy a new (used, but new to them) boat every year. There would be no high hotel or resort fees, as they could eat, sleep, and live on the boat for three months' time, and thereby enjoy a cost of living comparable to back home!

So, that's what they did. Craig and Laura worked a few summers to gather up extra cash, and when they had enough, they went online and bought their first boat a few weeks before the beginning of summer. They dealt with an agent in Greece who agreed to sell their boat for them at the end of the summer.

Some summers, they lost a little bit of money on the sale of the boat, while during others they made some extra; it didn't matter to them, because they lived the lifestyle of the rich and famous on the salaries of two teachers.

When they had kids, they simply saved some more money, and bought and sold bigger boats. Imagine spending your childhood summers sailing the Mediterranean, experiencing other cultures, learning new languages! I would say those experiences alone were worth three times what they spent on the boat each year.

They had incredible adventures, met fascinating people, made friends all over the world, and had fantastic stories to tell each fall upon returning to school.

Craig and Laura accomplished all this simply by thinking outside the box.

As you can see, you do not need to be wealthy to live a "working retirement." You just need to:

Want it
Plan for it
Realize it

As we saw with Craig and Laura, they had a strong desire to get more out of life. They wanted a change. They then sat down and planned how they could make that change: this is the step many of us fail to take. We all want more, but very few of us sit down and plan how to achieve it. Craig and Laura used skills they already had. Neither one had to go out, and learn and study to achieve this new found freedom. They simply looked inside themselves and found that they possessed it within.

Then they took the most important step of all: they realized their goal. So many of us want something, and some of us even start the planning process, but very few people actually take the gamble and follow through to realize those plans. Yet, that is where all the magic happens.

Let's do an exercise. What excites you in life? What gets you going? What dreams do you have? If you could do something fun and exciting, what would it be? Write these ideas down on the following page.

Next, what special skills do you have? Think hard on this one. Did you learn something as a child that you still enjoy doing today? Boating, fishing, going to the beach? Write down these skills as well.

Are there places you wish to visit? Adventures you want to experience? Write these down on the following blank lines.

Great, now let's see where any of these intersect. Maybe you are a real estate agent who loves the mountains. You could begin using your expert knowledge to locate some nice mountaintop land with a cabin and possibly acquire it at below market value.

Maybe you love to ski and your spouse is a real estate agent; great: combine the two to get a deal on a chalet near your favorite resort and ski for less money during your working years.

Maybe you love to travel and have a beautiful house. Put your house up on a house-swapping website. People will want to stay at your house, and you can stay at theirs free. Now the biggest expense is your travel; you've taken care of your lodging.

I believe there are endless ways that you can start living your retirement now, instead of waiting until that far off day. Getting more enjoyment out of life outside of work will increase your productivity on the job, reduce your stress, and help to make your relationships go smoother.

Life can be a wonderful time. My wife, Christine, and I love to travel. We started out saying we would make an effort to take a vacation every quarter. Christine didn't believe we could do it. She felt she could not get the time off and we couldn't afford it. Two years and nearly 20 vacations later, she is a true believer in the power of the process.

We wrote down our goals, figured out how to achieve them, and then we realized them. We blew the lid off our original goal of four vacations a year, and now we average almost one a month. I am far more productive at the office, my clients love hearing about all our travels, and our relationship has never been better.

This all did not happen on its own. We purposefully set out to make it a reality. We decided together that we wanted to practice a "working retirement." Our friends and coworkers can't believe it. They ask all the time, "How do you do it?" "Simple," I reply. "You need to want it, plan it, and then realize it." I think anything is possible once you set your mind to it.

Living a "working retirement" does not need to involve a lot of travel; you may simply want to make your hobbies a priority. If you love golfing, why wait until retirement to do more? Work actively to get out on the greens on a weekly basis. If you are in sales, get a membership to a local club, and take your clients out a couple times a week. There are more business deals done on the golf course than in the boardroom, in my opinion.

If you are passionate about cooking, sign up for local culinary classes, check out your local YMCA for group classes; take a culinary trip to Italy. You may find that these will enhance your appreciation of the culinary arts and make your working life more enjoyable.

I have worked with countless people who, when asked when they would like to retire, answer, "tomorrow." I could see the look in their eyes that told me they felt they would be happier if they didn't have to work at all. I would disagree. I think we as people need to have a purpose. Sure, they may not enjoy the job or career they have currently, but that doesn't mean they couldn't find something that makes them truly happy and allows them to get more out of life.

Maybe retirement should not be our final goal at all. Maybe it's the *idea* of retirement that keeps us going. The thought that one day we won't have to work anymore. Maybe that's all we really want. So let's focus not on our work, but on our passions. Our passions will be what fulfill us. It is what will make us get up every day, keep us going on those hard days, and reward us when we are enjoying them.

Passion is what we should be reaching for, not retirement.

Retire from work, but not from life
~ M. K. Soni ~

IMPORTANT RESOURCE REMINDER

I've put together a great set of resources for you that has been referenced in a few places throughout this book. My goal is to simply provide more information for you and to help you achieve your goals. There is NO FEE for this set of resources, it is my gift to you.

Simply go to

www.WirbickResource.com

and I'll be happy to give you access.

BONUS Reference Section:

Checklists and Questions

for Working with a Financial Advisor or Retirement Planning Professional:

Now that you have completed the book, you may naturally be asking yourself some questions such as:

Is this something I can do on my own?

If I wanted to hire someone how would I go about accomplishing that?

Once I book an appointment with an advisor how do I prepare?

What questions should I be asking?

I put this section together to help you answer these and many more questions, and to help you take the next action steps on your road to retirement.

First, refer back to chapter 2 to get some ideas of the type of advisor with which you would like to work.

Next, I would ask your friends and relatives if they have any experience working with someone they could recommend. If they give you a name, I would then go online and do some research to see if they meet your criteria before calling the company.

Once you have secured an appointment you will want to prepare some materials to take with you.

On the next few pages is a list of the items I like to see at a first meeting with a potential client. Generally, the more information you provide up front, the better the advice or guidance the advisor can give.

Suggested items to take with you for the first meeting with a professional advisor:

1. **Most recent Federal Tax Return**

   This allows the advisor to better understand where you are currently, what types of income you are receiving, and how they might be able to help you manage your tax situation in regards to investments.

2. **Retirement Statements**

   Bring along the most recent statements for any investments you may have. Include your 401k, IRA, Roth IRA. Bring the entire statement even if you do not think it is necessary.

3. **Brokerage Statement**

   Make sure to bring your most recent non-IRA statements.

4. **All Life Insurance Statements**

   A professional advisor will not just look at your investments. They will also analyze your insurances. It is important that you bring along the most recent annual statement and the actual policy. There is information that can be gained from both documents.

You may want to call the insurance company and request an "in – force illustration". This will give the advisor a good look into the health of your policy.

5. **Your Homeowner and Auto Insurance Statements**

   The advisor may not be licensed to sell these policies, and that is ok. They just need to verify that you have enough liability protection in place.

6. **Bank Statements**

   A current balance of you checking, savings, and money market accounts is important to ensure you have sufficient emergency cash.

7. **CD Statements**

   The advisor would want to see what rate you are currently receiving on your certificates of deposit. Make sure the statement lists the term and current interest rate.

8. **Long Term Care Policies**

   It is important that you have these reviewed every so often to make sure they are still meeting your needs.

9. **Goals**

It helps to write down what you want to accomplish at the meeting. This puts you and the advisor on the same page and may help you achieve your goals faster. I have provided some space here for you on the next page here to write down specifics on your own goals as you think of them.

GOALS:

____

____

____

____

____

____

____

____

____

____

____

10. List of Questions

A list of questions that you would like to ask. It is important that you and the advisor are on the same page when it comes to the goals you wish to accomplish. I have included a list of potential questions below that you may wish to ask. I always recommend that you write down these questions so nothing is missed. I am impressed when a new client comes in with an extensive list of questions. It shows they care about the process.

The following pages contain a list of questions you may want to ask at your first meeting. This is by no means an exhaustive list. However, it may help you to think of some other questions that may be important to you. I have included additional blank lines at the end for your convenience to add to this list.

Example Questions:

1. Are my current investments meeting my risk tolerance?

2. Am I invested too aggressively or too conservatively?

3. Are the fees I am paying currently in line with the industry?

4. Should I be investing in traditional or Roth IRAs?

5. Am I investing enough to meet my retirement goals?

6. Am I adequately insured, both for my life and for my possessions?

7. Do I have the right Life insurance for my needs?

8. Do I have the right level of Auto and Homeowners coverage?

9. Am I contributing enough at my company retirement plan?

10. How can I lower my taxes both now and in the future?

11. What option should I be considering for Social Security?

12. How will my IRA affect my taxes during my retirement?

13. How much inflation should I consider during my retirement years?

14. Should I consider Long Term Care Insurance?

15. What are the positives and negatives with traditional Long Term Care insurance?

16. Are there alternatives to Long Term Care insurance?

17. Should I have all investments in the Market?

18. How do I truly diversify my investments?

19. Should I be investing with an Active or a Passive money manager?

20. Will my tax bracket be higher or lower during my retirement years?

21. How will get money out of my retirement accounts to live on?

22. What assets should I spend down first?

23. Do I take Social Security first or spend my IRAs first?

24. Does it matter which assets I spend down first?

25. Am I investing my 401k properly for my risk tolerance?

26. What is my risk tolerance?

27. How do you establish my risk tolerance?

28. How do you get compensated?

29. How often would we meet?

30. How do you communicate with your clients?
31. Do you have any complaints registered against you?
32. How do you track whether we are on pace for success?
33. Do you personally use the investments that you recommend?
34. Are you affiliated with the companies you recommend?
35. Why do you want to work with us?

Additional Questions to Ask: